Our Changing Earth and Sky

Fabiola Sepulveda

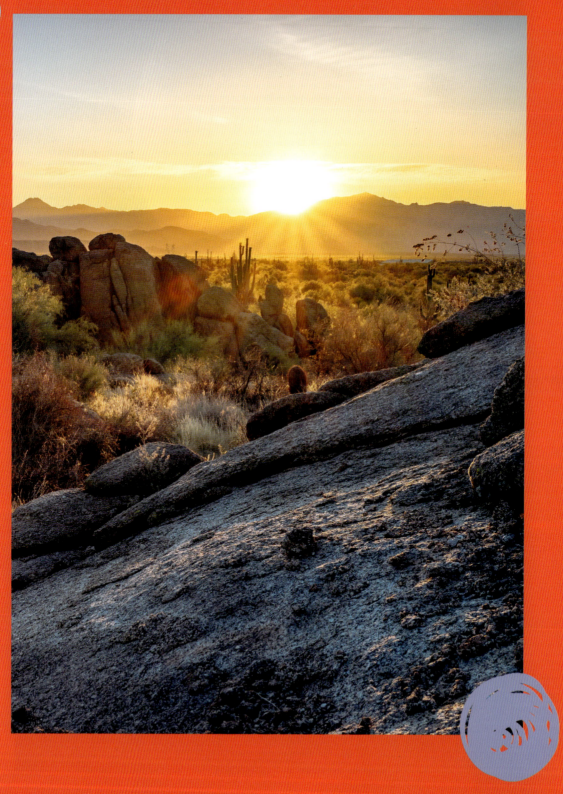

Notes for the Grown-ups

This wordless book allows for a rich shared reading experience for children who do not yet know how to read words or who are beginning to learn. Children can look at the pages to gather information from what they see, and they can suggest text to tell the story.

To extend this reading experience, do one or more of the following:

Draw pictures of Earth and sky changes, such as day and night.

Introduce vocabulary such as these words when looking at the pictures and telling the story you see:

- crescent
- erosion
- evaporation
- dry
- fall
- moon
- phase
- spring
- summer
- sun
- sunrise
- sunset
- tide
- wet
- winter

Talk about the changes you see in this book: erosion, seasons, tides, rain and evaporation, moon phases, and sunrise to sunset.

After reading the pictures, come back to the book again and again. Rereading is an excellent tool for building literacy skills.

Go outside and look for changes in the sky or on the earth. Moving clouds, wind, water flowing, leaves falling, and so on all indicate changes.

Consultant

Cynthia Malo, M.A.Ed.

Publishing Credits

Rachelle Cracchiolo, M.S.Ed., *Publisher*
Emily R. Smith, M.A.Ed., *SVP of Content Development*
Véronique Bos, *VP of Creative*
Dona Herweck Rice, *Senior Content Manager*

Image Credits: all images from iStock and/or Shutterstock

Library of Congress Cataloging in Publication Control Number:
2024012318

5482 Argosy Avenue
Huntington Beach, CA 92649
www.tcmpub.com
ISBN 979-8-7659-6151-3
© 2025 Teacher Created Materials, Inc.
Printed by: 926. Printed in: Malaysia. PO#: PO11723